The early poetry of
JOHN HENRIK CLARKE

Africa World Press, Inc.

P.O. Box 1892
Trenton, New Jersey 08607

REBELLION IN

RHYME

Africa World Press, Inc.

P.O. Box 1892
Trenton, New Jersey 08607

Copyright © 1991 John Henrik Clarke
Originally published by the Decker Press in 1948
First Africa World Press Edition 1991

Cover design and illustrations by Carles Juzang

Book design and typesetting by Malcolm Litchfield
This book is composed in Adobe Garamond and ITC Bauhaus

Library of Congress Catalog Card Number: 91-70748

ISBN: 0-86543-230-9   Cloth
        0-86543-231-7   Paper

CONTENTS

Encouragement

Love Cycle

Miscellaneous

DEDICATION

To Dr. Willis N. Huggins, friend and teacher, who spent a
life-time striving toward the realization of the kind of
humanity that we have so long dreamed about and
who taught me the political meaning of history.

and

To Evelina Taylor, my fifth-grade
teacher in the Columbus, Georgia Public
School System, who taught me to believe in myself.

INTRODUCTION

Most of the poems in this volume were written when I was between the age of 18, in the summer of 1933, and the age of 26, in the summer of 1941. These poems reflect my early beginnings as a social thinker and as a young man, straight out of the South during my early years in Harlem reflecting on the African condition and the awareness learned from associating with a diversity of politically-left movements and the revival of the Garvey Movement during the Italian-Ethiopian War, 1930–1936. I was a member of the Harlem History Club then functioning out of the Harlem YMCA on 135th Street. I was active in the National League of Negro Youth and, for a short period, in the Young Communist League. I was discovering the world and social change and wondering what role my people would play in the change for a better world. The writing of these poems at this juncture in my personal development was a form of therapy, a ventilation of my inner-self, an airing of my grievances and a celebration of the fact of my being alive. I developed a possessive love for my own people and their place in history at this time that was to stay with me for the rest of my life. During this period I became what I still am: a Socialist, a Pan-Africanist and an African World Nationalist. I have never seen any contradiction in being all of these simultaneously, and I have always maintained, and still do, that if other people see a problem in this they might, indeed, be the problem. In having love and commitment to my own people I have developed the same feeling for the whole of humankind—it was not difficult for me to learn that no one people's freedom is safe while another people's freedom is in danger.

Most of these poems were written on the spur of the moment, with little re-writing. When one is young and quite a few years away from thirty, this is how one approaches things. Except for two poems, Sing Me A New Song and Meditations Of A European

Farmer, all of these poems were written before I was inducted into the army in 1941, where I spent four years, two months and 26 days. The significance of the republication of these poems at this time is that a large number of my students, friends and colleagues do not know that I ever wrote poetry and are curious to know what kind of poetry I did write if indeed I did write poetry. The final reason is that the republication of these poems allows me to observe the progression of my thinking over the last fifty years—measuring the distance between where I started and where I am now as a Teacher, Intellect and a committed African Freedom Fighter.

JOHN HENRIK CLARKE

Professor Emeritus
African World History
Dept. of Africana & Puerto Rican Studies
Hunter College, N.Y.

October, 1990

IN PROTEST

IN PROTEST

A Question to the Warriors

If you are the noble and brave
Who have great harvest to reap,
Why do you cowardly fling death at night
While babies sleep?

Meditations of a European Farmer

Where now shall I lay my head?
The fields which once yielded me
Both shelter and bread,
Are now odored with rotting dead.
Since that horde of strangers
Trampled upon my land
Planting both dead flesh and lead,
I wonder will the fields ever again
Yield eatable bread.

Inquiry

How can you sing America?
With your souls baptized in glee,
Advertising your greatness,
Boasting of your victories,
While men denied justice,
Are hanging from your trees?

Sing Me a New Song

Sing me a new song, young black singer,
Sing me a song with some thunder in it,
And a challenge that will
Drive fear into the hearts of those people
Who think that God has given them
The right to call you their slave.

Sing me a song of strong men growing stronger
And bold youth facing the sun and marching.
Sing me a song of an angry sharecropper,
Who is not satisfied with his meager share
Of the produce that he squeezed from the earth
While watering the earth with his sweat and tears.

Sing me a song of two hundred million Africans,
Revising the spirit of Chaka, Moshesk and Menelik,
And shouting to the world:
"This is my land and I shall be free upon it!"
Put some reason in my song and some madness too.

Let the reason be the kind of reason
Frederick Douglas had,
When he was fighting against slavery in America.
Let the madness be the kind of madness
Henri Christophe had when
He was driving Napoleon's army from Haitian soil.

Sing me a song with some hunger in it, and a challenge too.
Let the hunger be the kind of hunger
Nat Turner and Denmark Vesey had,
When they rose from bondage and inspired
Ten thousand black hands to reach for freedom.

Let the challenge be the kind of challenge
Crispus Attucks had
While dying for American Independence.

Don't put "I ain't gonna study war no more"
in my song.
Sing me a song of people hungry for freedom,
Who will study war until they are free!

Love

Who is justice? I would like to know,
Whosoever she is, I could love her so.
I could love her, though my race
So seldom looks upon her face.

Desire

I'd like to hear music
In the whisper of the wind
But the roar of cannons drowns it out . . .
And the sound of marching men.
I'd like to smell the flowers
As the wind blows through my hair,
But men are dying on battle fields . . .
And their odor fills the air.

The Mother Speaks

When the bugles blow again
Calling men to fight,
When the wise men speak again,
About what is wrong and what is right,
I will not turn listening ears
Toward those who led men to slaughter;
I will blankly refuse to hear
When the cannons call for more fodder.
For them I have no joyous cheers,
No hands to grip their guns,
I'll give a chorus of forceful jeers
But I will not give my son.

Shame

I could not look upon her face,
'Twas agony-ridden beyond compare,
I thought only of the disgrace
That put the agony there.
I viewed the sight, then asked aloud,
"O God, why should this be?"
Her son hangs on yonder tree;
I could not look upon her face
Without thinking of her hectic plight,
I turned my back on this sight.
Overhead a flock of stars were
Smiling like a lovely dancer;
She lifted her hands and called
A God that did not answer.

Explanation

A smile of hope
And a frown of despair,
A hangman's rope
And a scornful stare;
This, too, is America, you see,
But not what America was meant to be.

Interlude

A dark girl entered a white man's church
To bow in meditation
She found nought but scornful stares
From the waiting congregation.
A white man rose and uttered:
"Dear maiden, can't you see that you are dark
And I am white ... you cannot worship here with me."
She stood aghast with tear-filled eyes,
And with an air of dread
She looked outward at the skies,
And this is what she said:
"He calls himself a christian,
As he goes here and there
But he forbids a dark girl
To bow with him in prayer."

Fools Unaware

'Twas more than a man hung,
Unjustly, on Georgia's tree.
With that man unconsciously
They hung humanity.
'Twas more than an odor that passed,
When the wind blew through the trees
'Twas justice dead and withered ...
Like a heap of Autumn leaves.

No Tears

Shed no tears for the strong nations
Now crumbling ...
Shout gleefully as they fall!
The next great glory will belong to the people
Who have lived so long
Without any glory at all.

The Summons

Africans, now that the usurper of your
Power is busy in battle with usurpers,
Lift again your spear and shield
And reclaim the land that was yours
When time was young.
Thrust your dusty chest forward and shout ...!
Murderer, yes, proud murderer,
Murderer for freedom!

Two Ladies

I saw two ladies pass by,
That earned the attention of me.
One was scorned bitterly
The other treated with courtesy.
Both were beautifully adorned
In silks and laces.
The only difference between them
Was the color of their faces.

Black Rhapsody

Our rhapsody is made of tears
Long held back from our eyes,
The tedious burdens of troubled years
And long submerged sighs.
Yet, we come, bearing neither
Contempt nor retort.
The running tears have washed
The malice from our hearts.

American Scene

They hurled him into a courtroom
Of merciless men.
The odds were against him
Before the trial began.
To convict the man accused,
Sufficient evidence they lacked.
They couldn't let him go
Without being abused;
So, they convicted him for being black.

Sound in the Dark — 1935

There was no fallacy
In this sound I heard,
This sound, that was not a sound
Yet, more distinct than
The spoken word.
It was a bewildered Ethiopian
Crying at the tomb of Menelik . . .
Longing for leadership
In a confused world.

II HIS CRY

Menelik! Wake up Menelik;
This is not time to sleep,
Can't you hear the angry trod
Of the invader's feet?
This is not time to rust,
Ancient Ethiopia is being
Trampled in the dust.

A Plea: and a Protest

I heard Africa cry
Bearing the burden of these years.
I did not hear a single sigh
And no one wiped her tears.
I saw Africa bleed.
They robbed her of her best,
And no one saw the need
To wipe the blood from her breast.

Note to a White Man

Yes, I cleaned your boots:
I rubbed them hard
So they could shine,
And when you spoke
I said, "Yes Sir,"
As if you were some great "Divine."

Now, turn back
The pages of history.
In there, a place
You'll find,
Where I didn't clean your boots,
But you cleaned mine.

Lines Written at the Grave of the Unknown Soldier

Walk softly, do not make a sound,
Cautiously your feet must touch the ground.
Take heed; are you not aware
The "Unknown Soldier" is sleeping here?
When passing you must carefully creep.
Do not disturb his lasting sleep.
He fought to give us better things . . .
He must know he fought in vain.
Don't awaken him, for fear he see
That we have destroyed democracy.

EXPLANATIONS

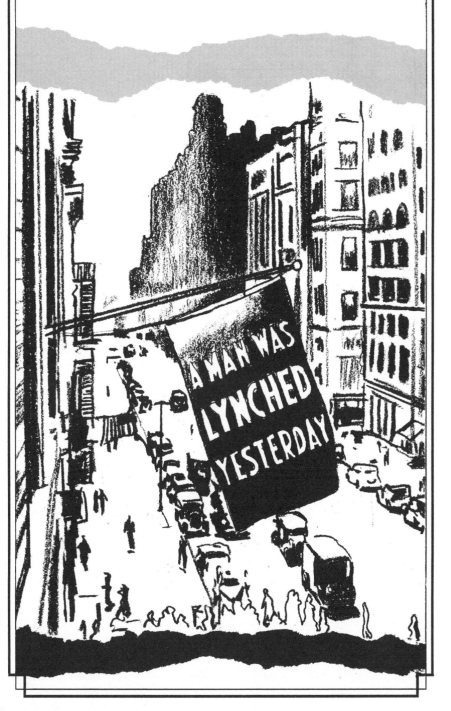

EXPLANATIONS

The Poet Speaks

I know there seem to be
Little reason or rhyme
For the men who write of beauty
In such conflicting times . . .
But I am one of those men
Who strive to yield
Golden fruit from a stone field.

Shockproof

With strong nations buckling at the knees,
And zealots claiming victories,
I would not be shocked if the stars
Flew away like a swarm of bees.
And if the grass long green
Should suddenly turn pink before my eyes,
I would not be surprised.

The City's Conquest

The city has conqured me
Though it causes me pain.
I love it's bewitching spell
That's rampant in my veins.
No matter how hungrily I long
For laughing seas,
And quiet rural charms,
I will not relinquish the city's might
To roam over wooded lands,
And sleep through silent nights.

Request

When I am approaching my journey's end
This I ask of those who call me friend . . .
Do not mourn or weep over me,
Just sigh a brief sigh of thoughtfulness
And say, "he will soon be free."
When my burdened heart
Has ceased to throb,
Do not cry my dears,
Keep your muted sobs,
Keep your salty tears.

Confession

I sing of tranquility in a troubled world.
In the midst of wars, I sing of peace.
When rain comes, I sing of the sun.
To demagogues I sing the Golden Rule.
I am a poet, and a fool.

Poem

I heard one doubtful mortal say,
"Beauty no longer dwells in our day,
Bells of joy no longer ring,
And friendship is a forgotten thing."
Ah, if he would but walk
At midnight . . .
And listen to the song
That the midnight sings.

Then and Now

When I was a little boy,
About half past three,
All the world was a garden to me.
Rain and other things from the sky
Was the grace of God passing by ...
But now, I bow my head and sigh,
As bombs fall and babies cry.
In a world wreathed in wild confusion,
I have lost every trace of my beautiful illusion.

Determination

My feet have felt the sands
Of many nations,
I have drunk the water
Of many springs.
I am old,
Older than the Pyramids,
I am older than the race
That oppresses me.
I will live on ...
I will out-live oppression,
I will out-live oppressors.

Caution

America is a young
And restless nation,
Young like a school girl,
Restless like a year old colt.
Those who guide her
Must guide her cautiously,
As if guiding a child.

Admitted with Regret

Gone is Babylon and the men
Who erected it, have long since
Faded into insignificance ...
While the men who ruled it
Live splendidly on
In the pages of history.
The Egypt of Cleopatra, along with
Cleopatra and all her beauty,
Have long since faded into dust,
And fertiled Egyptian soil,
That is yesterday,
And yesterday is but dust.
We of today are but
The dust of tomorrow.

Bombardment and Aftermath

The night passed over
And the day was born
Amid the rumble of man's eternal wrong . . .
This tragedy dwarfed every smile;
Silenced every song.
There was nothing but scattered pity
In this grotesque place,
That once was a city.

Poem

I'll tell you what nature says
When she whispers in my ear each day,
'Tis woven in each song she sings ...
"Man compared with me
Is an insignificant thing."

The Deserter

I cannot change worlds,
Nor can I prop them
When they start to fall;
Hence, I have no place
In this present tumult.
I will not exhaust my weak voice,
Or raise my frail hand,
But instead, I will stand
Far removed from danger and sing ...
(Like a bird in the wilderness)
To the glorification of nature,
And the damnation of man.

Truth

John Brown's body lies a molding
In the grave.
John Brown's body lies a molding
In the dust.
His truth goes marching on ...
But not quite fast enough.

Prediction

Some will mourn me.
Yes, I know,
Some will be sad
When I am no more.
Some will rejoice,
Like fools rejoice,
Glad to see me go.
Some will say
Like fools would say,
In voices gleeful
Like the bells:
There goes the atheist poet
On his way to hell.

A Prayer for Our Times

O God, send the rain,
Let it flood the battle fields,
Absorb the blood and ease the pain.
Probably man will again be sane;
O God, send the rain!

O God, send the snow,
Let it choke the cannon's roar.
From the wars, men will go
Back to the ones who love them so.
O God, send the snow!

O God, send the wind,
Let it blow away our sin,
Usurp the odor of dying men;
Then with music let it blind,
O God, send the winds!

O God, send the ice,
Let it freeze each crude device,
That man has to plunder life.
I ask no more, this will suffice.
O God, send the ice!

They Like to See Me Laugh

(THE VOICE OF A NEGRO LABORER)

They like to see me laugh, though the
Sweat runs from my brow,
And my limbs are tired from labor,
Labor that I must do somehow.
Hard and tiresome labor, that starts
When the day begins
And when these weary episodes are over,
They like to see me grin.
A gay and blushing smile upon my face,
They like to see, but they never stop to wonder
What goes on inside of me.
I bear a heavy burden
And sad as this may sound,
To them, my face must never wrinkle,
I must never wear a frown.
The journey I travel is weary
And I am very much displeased,
But for the sake of their amusement
I must pretend to be at ease.
They've thrown a screen around my past,
My former glory I must not see
With instruments of brutality,
They've buried my history.
This doesn't end my weary story,
You have yet to hear its half,
And through this entanglement
Of miserable sadness,
They like to see me laugh.

Babylon Is Not Dead

No, Babylon is not dead,
I saw Babylon yesterday,
In the grinning face of a red-cap
In Pennsylvania Station.
And later in the movements
Of a dark girl's body in a cabaret.
And only last night, I saw Babylon
Preaching against race hatred
From a step-ladder on Lenox Avenue.
No, Babylon is not dead;
I heard Babylon when a dark girl sang,
"I'm so glad my troubles won't last always."
Babylon is in the oppressed races
Rising from under the yoke of oppression;
Perhaps Babylon did sleep for a while,
But Babylon never died—
This is the day of Babylon's awakening.

No Age for Roses

This no age for roses,
The air is filled
With rank fallacies—
And reason is dead
As last season's leaves.
With men struggling desperately
To keep alive,
How can roses thrive?

America

I love this arrogant young nation,
Who parades her glory
Like a saucy maiden in a new dress . . .
I am warmed by its bigness
And strengthened by its zest.
In spite of its short-comings
And its over-rated might,
I will not yield one inch of it
Without a fight.

Poem

Being neither philosopher or sooth-sayer,
I can not solve the problems
Of this dismal day;
I can neither free a mortal from fear,
Nor hold an army at bay.
So, I shall flee, like a wild gypsy,
Out to the woods and play.

Foresight

When I have viewed my last day
And still in the death chamber I lay,
My kinsmen will come from far and near
And shower me with praises I can no longer hear,
And some who suppose to have loved me well,
Will bring me flowers I can no longer smell.

When the world has forgotten the place of my birth
And my grave has sunk even with the earth,
Many mortals not knowing that I am buried there
Will walk over me with gleeful grace,
And they will be unaware
That they are walking on my face.

Pagan as I Am

Pagan as I am, I understand,
There's something vitally wrong
With the present order of things.
Treaties are but mere scraps of paper,
And trust has lost its meaning.
Pagan as I am, I often say,
We cannot go this way.

Prophecy

When they bury my noble remains
In the bosom of this earth:
The underground bugs will eat my brain
Thru' them, I'll have a rebirth.
And they will become the wisest of bugs—
Across their world they'll fly.
With life's great problems they will not tug
'Cause they will be wiser than I.

Sad Child

I am a strange child,
In a strange land;
The West is neither my
Home nor my haven.
My music is the 'tom-tom'
Not the Saxophone,
You may root me here
In this alien soil,
But I will not grow.
I may never go back to
The East, where I belong;
But I will forever nurse the desire.
In the hours when I am alone,
I'll turn my pagan face toward
The East, and cry.

Changing Times

Yesterday, only fools cast
Bread upon the waters;
Today, alleged "wise men,"
Seemingly with an insane passion
To outstrip fools,
Are freely casting human beings.

Lines — June, 1939

When Spain cried out for mercy,
A million hands were outstretched,
A million prayers were said—
Where are the hands?
Where are the prayers?
Now that Spain is dead.

Time to Die

Before my face is pale and wrinkled
And my hair is thin and gray,
Before my limbs are weak and withered,
I'd like to pass away.

I want not to live
'Till I am too old to rise
And greet the dawn;
And friends pitifully say,
"There goes old John."

I'd like to live like a flower;
Fresh as a new-born day,
Before all of my freshness has faded,
I'd like to pass away.

I'd like to die before my eyes are weak
And I'm bent down with strife.
When I can no longer see my way,
I've had enough life.

A Threat

After my noble bones have decayed,
And my name is less than a name,
In the vast sea of forgotten things,
I will roam this earth again,
But not in the form of a man.
Villain-like, my dust will lurk in corners,
And wait 'till people come by;
Then for the sheer hell of it,
I shall blow into every eye.

Lines — June, 1938

Reason and rain is
Greatly needed in Spain.
Reason, to bring men
Home from the trenches,
Philosophy to bridle their sins,
Rain, to wash away the blood,
When the smoke of battle has thinned.

Spring Morning

I saw a bird flutter from its nest
Singing with sweet delight,
There was a newborn freshness,
On everything in sight.
My soul was raptured over and over,
And all the world was right.
Most beautiful of all I saw ...
The morning steal out of the night.

We: the Versemakers

We preserve troubles, heartaches and snares,
Cruelty, kindness and petty love affairs;
And some of the nicer things we've heard
Are sculptured in fancy words.
We look beyond many rising suns,
And give the world beauty that's yet to come.
When the curtain falls on our lives
We receive no great ovation ...
Fate has granted us but few mortals,
To bow in humble consideration.

Admiration

I love the night because it is
Dark like my face ...
Dark and deep enough to
Absorb the sorrows that infest the day,
Motherly and kind enough to nurse
This heart of mine, that has
So long been burdened with pain.
O God, if you ever want this insignificant
Body of mine ... tear it into a million bits
And fling it far into the night,
So I may never again hear the sorrowful
Cries of my people, pleading for justice.
Let me never again hear the ugly cry
Of race and creed.

Child of the Earth

Matters not where on earth you take me,
When Spring-time comes along
I'll always feel a yearning
For green and tasseling corn.
I belong to the faithful earth,
And some day I will have a bed
In the ever faithful earth—
That gives us bread.

ENCOURAGEMENT

Challenge

The west has been won;
It has served its days of woe;
The pioneers have laid down their guns
Now, where can the young men go!

Young men, I have an answer,
You need not sit and whine;
Arise and build a haven
For the disinherited of mankind.

The Call

Come now strong bodied Zulu,
Come Ethiopian from your mountain cage,
Come seize the reins of power;
Restore it to its rightful place.
Come and give the world some reason,
Come with calmness, not with rage ...
Come, lift the banner of righteousness;
Africa, this is your age.

Encouragement

Be not dismayed my brothers.
This tension piercing the air
Is neither destruction,
Nor the seeds of destruction ...
Echoes of this present strife
Are but the infant—future,
Restless in the womb of life.

Hope in the Crisis

This not the end of all good things;
There will be more smiles and joyful songs ...
This is just the dark hour
That comes before the dawn.

Hope

This I say to those who in dark hours
Fear that the end of all that is
Stout and good is near,
And the forces of right and noble
Hath fallen to the rear.

"In spite of man's savage folly
And the disasters that it brings,
Hope will emerge triumphantly
With a new song to sing."

When the odor of war no longer
Pollutes the wind,
And the cries of hate have met their doom,
When the heinous smoke of battle has thinned
Perhaps some flowers will bloom.

Forward to Present-Day Negro Youth

Forward, always forward, forward is the command;
Look not on dead yesterday,
A present battle is at hand.
Raise your voice in splendid tones,
So sleeping men can hear!
Don't be a backslider in the ranks,
Be a pioneer.
Don't hold behind your lips,
Words that you wish to say;
Dip your torch in the oils of courage;
Light it and lead the way.

I know your burden is heavy
And your goal seems not in sight,
Travel on with your heavy burden
And your weary road will lead to light.
Forward along life's rugged road,
Believing that right is might;
When the road seems dark ahead of you,
Self-confidence will be your light.

Even if it seems that your weary path
Is hidden from the sun,
Never lay down your weapon
Until the battle is won.
Again I say, forward,

Forward like fighting men:
Though life's mountains are steep and rugged,
With courage you can ascend.
With that you cannot fail;
Other men will rise with eagerness,
To follow your fearless trail.

Lines of Encouragement

I know what you're thinking,
Little black boy with rusty feet;
Let not your hopes be shrinking,
Let not your mind dwell indigent.
I hope you are tired of the dusty cotton fields
And toiling 'til day is done.
For you, you want your strength to yield
A place in the sun.
I know you want your well-earned chance
To taste the sweets of victory.
The world now views you with a dismal glance,
But this won't always be.

Encouragement II

Beyond the dark horizon,
Beyond the mass of glum,
If we can see a little hope
We can see the sun.
If we can mend our broken hearts
Hugging courage from despair,
Then we can grasp a brave new start,
And fight our way to anywhere.
We've suffered from the lack of might,
Yet we have survived the darkest day;
Now all we need is a little light
And we will find our way.

A Fragment of Hope

Go on little man,
Dream your dreams,
Hurl your hopes
Toward the sky.
Some will flourish
In splendid gleam
Before you die.
Dream a multitude of dreams;
Surely they'll not all come true;
Futile as this may seem,
You'll realize a scattered few.

LOVE CYCLE

A Portrait

FOR MARION E. TANNER

She walked into the garden
When the day was fresh and new,
And the sky was just adorning
Her dress of royal blue.
When the birds saw her footsteps,
Through the fading dawn,
They paused in humble reverence
And sang their sweetest song.
The wind marveled at this wonderful thing,
A newborn flower, leaning forward
To kiss the Spring.

An Explanation

FOR ORA M. INGRAM

I would like to remember
Your well balanced grace,
And the noble stamp of spring
Upon your face ...
But time has not soothed
The torturing lust
Of our parting hours,
When I asked for flowers,
And you gave me dust.

Poem

I dream of a maiden so kind, so fair
And fresh as the flowers at morn,
Blessed with beauty beyond compare,
And once I called her my own.
But death thought her too good for me,
And snatched her from my midst,
She lives on in my memory,
But only the earth can share her kiss.

Forlorn

I have naught, but night;
Since time erased your name,
Since death stretched her pale hands forward
And sang a mute refrain.

Interracial

She said she didn't love him,
Because he was black and she was white;
She met him in the dark
She wouldn't dare meet him in the light.
She said she despised him,
But after he was gone ...
They found her weeping sadly
On his cold tombstone.

Poem

You came after my heart had been broken
So completely, it could never be mended.
And I had sworn to the Gods of romance
Never to love again.

I had been faithful to a previous one,
Who crushed my heart for the sake of fun,
When you came and offered true love,
I had not the strength to respond.

So go away and let me be;
And behind you close the gate,
I could have loved you passionately—
Only you came too late.

If We Must Part

If we must part,
Let it be now, now, while
Our love is garish and real ...
And the place you have
In my heart can in time
Be refilled.
If your love cannot survive,
Until my last day,
Then gather your belongings
And go your way.
Don't wait 'til I am old and gray
When the thought of losing you
Will slowly eat my heart away.

Faded Love

Her face was sad when we
Met that night,
Her previous pleasantness, was left behind.
I foretold from her action
That something vital was on her mind.
The stars above did not inspire,
The bright new moon she did not see.
She was no longer gay and amusing
As she used to be;
Our beautiful love had faded,
That I could very well see.
In a sad tone she said "good night,"
I knew she no longer cared for me.

I'm from Alabama

I'm from Alabama—red clay still
On m' feet,
I gitta gal 'n' Alabama, who lives
On de Chinaberry rout;
Yeh, I'm from Alabama
An' dat's nothing t' brag about.
Gon' sent fer m' gal 'n' Alabama,
So she kin marry me;
Gonna brang dat gal t' Harlem
An' how happee we gonna be.
Gonna build her a house on "Sugar Hill,"
Where day's never feelin' low;
Yeh, I'm from Alabama,
But I ain't goin' back no more.

In Love

I am in love with each twig of grass
That grows around my feet,
And the blessed breezes that pass
Forever kissing my cheeks.
I watch the days come and go
Inspiration into my heart they hurl;
I adore the sun and its splendid glow,
I am in love with the whole wide world.

Reminiscence

I gave her a kiss, a passionate kiss
And warmly she did thank me.
I gave her a rose, a red, red rose,
A rose her eyes were glad to see.
I declared my love in flowery terms,
Her eyes lit up with joyous beams;
When I awakened she was gone,
I must have wooed her in my dreams.

Tribute

Dark little maiden scampering along
Like a flower running wild;
I love your face,
I love your song,
I love your simple style.
Dark little maiden, do you not know
That you are nature's fairest child?

Two of a Kind

One dismal evening I met her
By a harbor wearily weeping,
I could not share her burden
Because sorrow into my heart was seeping.
From behind her tears forced a smile,
Gaiety from me, she sought to borrow,
I informed her in my best style
That my heart too was overrun with sorrow.

MISCELLANEOUS

A Plea

Come now gentle rain
The leaves are singing a song of pain;
Come and soothe their thirsty hours.
Come now gentle rain,
There's dust upon the flowers.

Tribute

O Gypsies, carefree children with simple grace,
You are the freest of human race.
You've built no towering skyscrapers ...
You wear no worries on your face.
To you I turn for comfort,
With tears devoid of glee,
O Gypsies, take all or part of me,
Press it passionately against your wild flesh
And make it free.

Depressed

I am sad tonight;
The world seems weary;
My tired mind longs for rest;
My books, my chair,
My other belongings,
My loneliness.
All around me
Life is gloomy;
Across my mind
Sad memories wave;
I think that every
Breath I'm breathing
Draws me closer
To the grave.

Lines of Tribute

FOR JAMES WELDON JOHNSON

I

He has neither been conquered nor subdued.
His dreams did not perish when he passes by,
Let us march forward with hope renewed
The banners of his army are still flying high.

II

Noble singer of noble songs,
Gallant crusher of many wrongs,
Our lives are brighter this day,
Because you came this way.

III

I don't think our tribute to this strong soldier,
Who never wept, not even when the battle
Was the most difficult, should be in tears.
Instead, let us dedicate our lives to finishing
The great work that he started.
And when we at last march into that
Long awaited new day, let us march
So gallantly, that he will know
We are marching.

Adieu Forever

Farewell passing day;
You have served your purpose.
You were no better or worse
Than any of the others;
Now you must end
Like all things must end,
And we must go our separate ways.
Soon You will be resting
In the grave of yesterday.

A Little Girl Speaks of Her Story Book

My book is like a friend to me,
It takes me way across the sea;
It educates and entertains me;
It drives my sadness all away.
When I sit down to read at the end of a day,
It takes me over hills and plains,
And many times to foreign lands
Where they speak languages, I don't understand.
When I turn another page,
I'm back home again:
Now, I've sailed the seven seas,
I've plucked foreign flowers,
I've seen the music-loving Viennese
All within an hour.
When the evening bows to night,
The clock on the wall I hear,
Then, much to my surprise,
I've never moved out of my chair.
It seems I've been away from home
When I take a backward look,
But the beautiful land in which I roamed,
Was all within my book.

Dream

The gates of Heaven were opened,
And angels rushed to meet me,
There were smooth roads of joy
As far as I could see;
The smiles on their faces
Were bright as the sun's beam;
My clock alarmed;
'Twas break of day
And I awakened from the dream.

Rejoice After Death

Lady rejoice and not mourn ...
Now that your no-good husband is gone,
You should celebrate and be gay,
Since that old drunkard passed away.
Not one tear should you unreel,
Not one moment should you mourn.
Throw him in some deserted field.
Maggots will eat the meat from his bones.

To a Magnolia

You look so restful and kind
Lovely flower of Spring,
Without a mind to think evil thoughts,
Or eyes to see evil things.
I wish I were like you
Lovely Magnolia,
Smiling in the early morn;
Unlike Humans, you die
As sinless as you were born.

Hatred

I hate winter, when birds migrate
And flowers die ...
When nights are long and filled with gloom,
And lovers no longer see the moon;
When nature's bright-faced children are dead,
And Jack Frost shows his ugly head,
Then I sit by the open fire
And watch the weary days go by.
I hate winter, when birds migrate
And flowers die.

Question

Where go the castles and armoured knights,
The dancing girls with eyes of blue?
Ask me not 'cause I never knew,
Where go the dreams that never come true.

Simple Puzzle

She has the kindest voice I ever heard,
She answers to a well-known
Six letter word . . .
To me she has the loveliest of charm;
An artist would paint her
With a child in her arms.
Somehow she stands out
From all the rest . . .
Yes, it's my mother, you don't have to guess.

When Father Sits Down to Read

When Father sits down to read,
It's quiet all around.
No one would dare whisper,
Or even make a sound.
He doesn't read about everyday things
Like flowers and shady nooks;
He always reads a story
From the greatest of story books.
Somehow he reads it most
In his darkest hours.
This wonderful book he loves so well,
Is the "Holy Bible."

Questions

Does death mean I'll depart
To some quiet place of rest,
And no longer I'll see human beings
Perish from the want of kindness?

Does death mean my eyes will be closed
To all brutal things,
And no longer I'll hear men
Pleading for justice in vain?

If death means I'll depart:
And agony I'll no longer see,
Then I greet death with all my heart;
O' death, I welcome thee.

My Queen

My queen is the most charming thing
As she sits on my knee;
She never argues about politics,
Nor how this world should be.

Nowhere has she an enemy,
And she always sings of glee;
To me she is the most precious of things,
And she is only three.

On Passing an Old Lady's Home

I passed by and saw them sitting there
Like withered and forlorn flowers;
Dreaming of days that once were rare,
While waiting for the final hour.
The grim curtain of age has fallen
Upon their lives that once were gay;
Stories of childhood pleasantness they tell ...
While waiting for death to take them away.

Poem

When leaves hang sleepily
From the trees,
And no sound is heard
Not even the hum of busy bees,
I creep quietly from my cottage
Into the glowing moonlight
And steal some lines for a sonnet
Out of the stillness of the night.

Dad

Many times Dad wrote me
Since away I roamed,
Somewhere in every letter he'd say,
"Son, please come home,"
When at last I decided
To consider his plea
And come home as he said;
I received a sad message
Explaining that Dad was dead.

Evening on the Farm

In the quiet winter evenings,
When the dreary shadows fall,
From a tree top of the nearby woods
I heard a robin call.
His songs of cheer and laughter
Make my troubles fade away,
And they always sound sweetest
At the end of a Winter day.

Poem

I stood in the silence of midnight,
Sucking comfort from the wind,
Wondering how long will God
Forgive man and his sins.
I heard a gentle murmur
Drifting from the starry sky;
Then I wept for the world,
As I kissed the night good-bye.

A Day: Dying

As if an angel had requested
It to sleep thrice and ten thousand hours
The sun retreated from the sky
And the gray of evening kissed the flowers.

The worn day is fading
Like an aging maiden pleading for pity ...
Now, night has come with ominous arms
To embrace the city.

A Withered Rose

A rose lay withered on the ground . . .
Its petals have long lost their sweet,
'Tis such a pity, that this
Beautifier of life
Will soon be trampled by human feet.
Though the rose has lived its life,
The joys of summer have gone by,
'Tis a sad, but true thing to say,
Roses like humans must live and die.